Albert Einstein

SADDLEBACK
EDUCATIONAL PUBLISHING

Saddleback's Graphic Biographies

SADDLEBACK
EDUCATIONAL PUBLISHING
www.sdlback.com

ISBN-13: 978-1-59905-212-0
ISBN-10: 1-59905-212-1
eBook: 978-1-60291-575-6

Printed in Singapore

19 18 17 16 15   6 7 8 9 10

·ALBERT EINSTEIN·

Albert Einstein was born in Germany in 1879. He became famous as a scientist and as one of the most important thinkers of our times. In 1933 when the dictator Adolph Hitler came to power in Germany, Einstein left his native land for good. Einstein was a Jew. Hitler hated Jews. In 1940 Albert Einstein became a citizen of the United States.

Although he made many important discoveries, he is best known for his theory of relativity. This law became the most famous equation in science. It read $E=mc^2$. "E" stands for energy, "m" stands for matter, and "c" stands for the speed of light multiplied by itself.

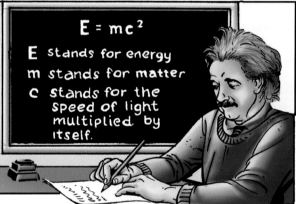

$$E = mc^2$$

E stands for energy
m stands for matter
c stands for the speed of light multiplied by itself.

One day when five-year old Albert was ill, his father bought him a gift.

My son, I have bought you a compass.

What's it for?

No matter how you hold it, the iron needle always points north. Sailors use it to find their way on the ocean.

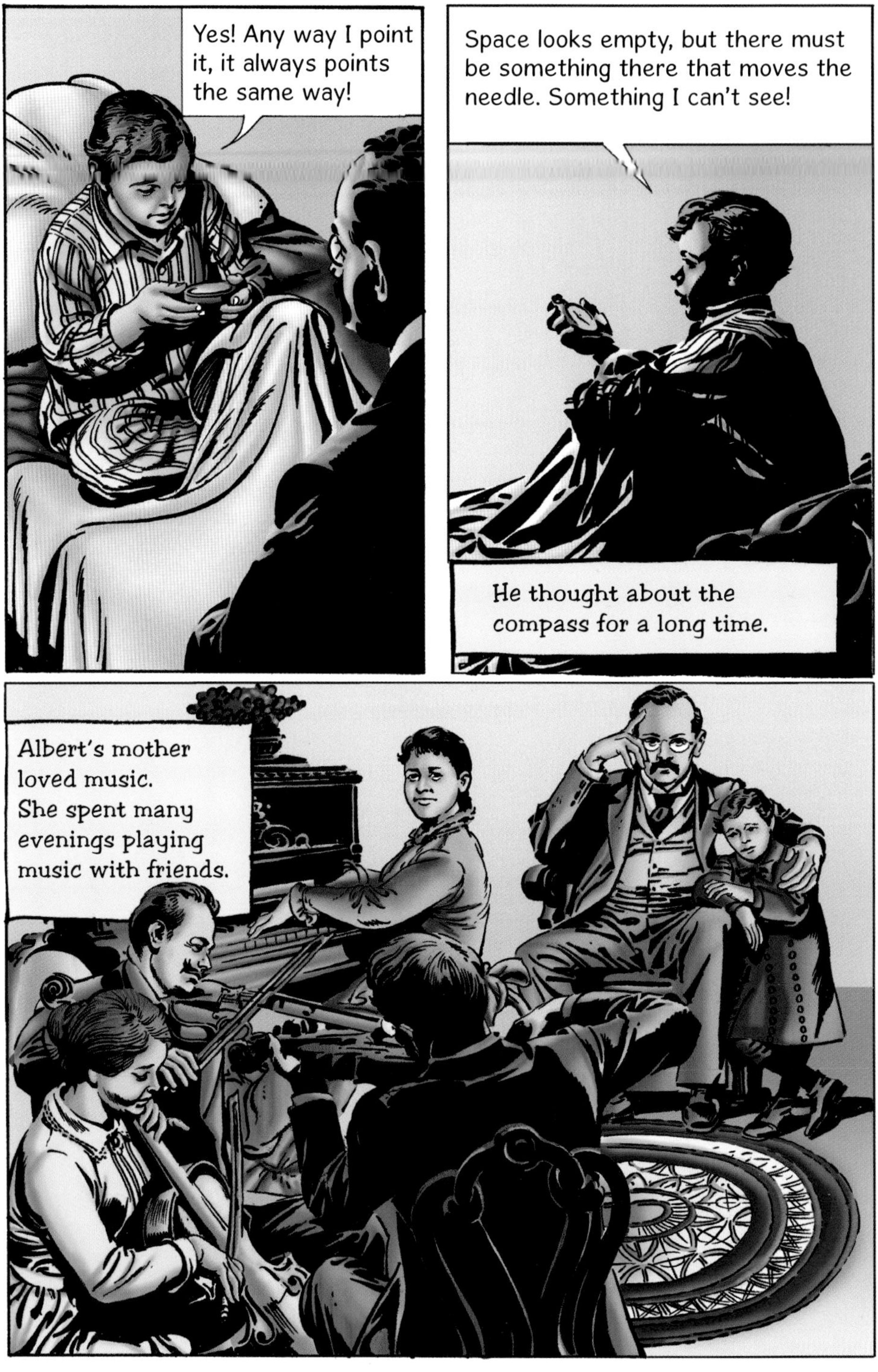
Yes! Any way I point it, it always points the same way!
Space looks empty, but there must be something there that moves the needle. Something I can't see!
He thought about the compass for a long time.
Albert's mother loved music. She spent many evenings playing music with friends.

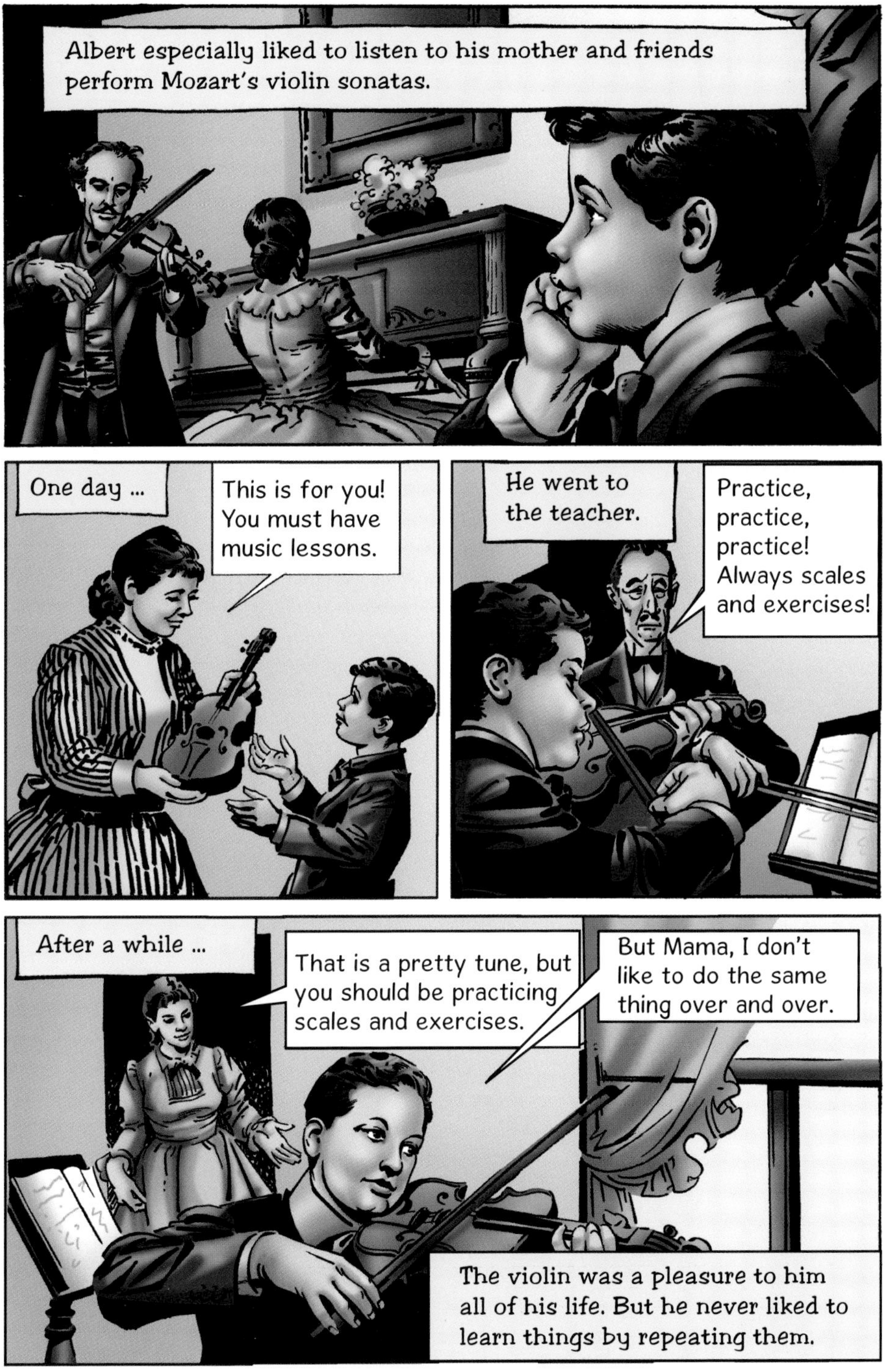
Albert especially liked to listen to his mother and friends perform Mozart's violin sonatas.
One day ...
This is for you! You must have music lessons.
He went to the teacher.
Practice, practice, practice! Always scales and exercises!
After a while ...
That is a pretty tune, but you should be practicing scales and exercises.
But Mama, I don't like to do the same thing over and over.
The violin was a pleasure to him all of his life. But he never liked to learn things by repeating them.

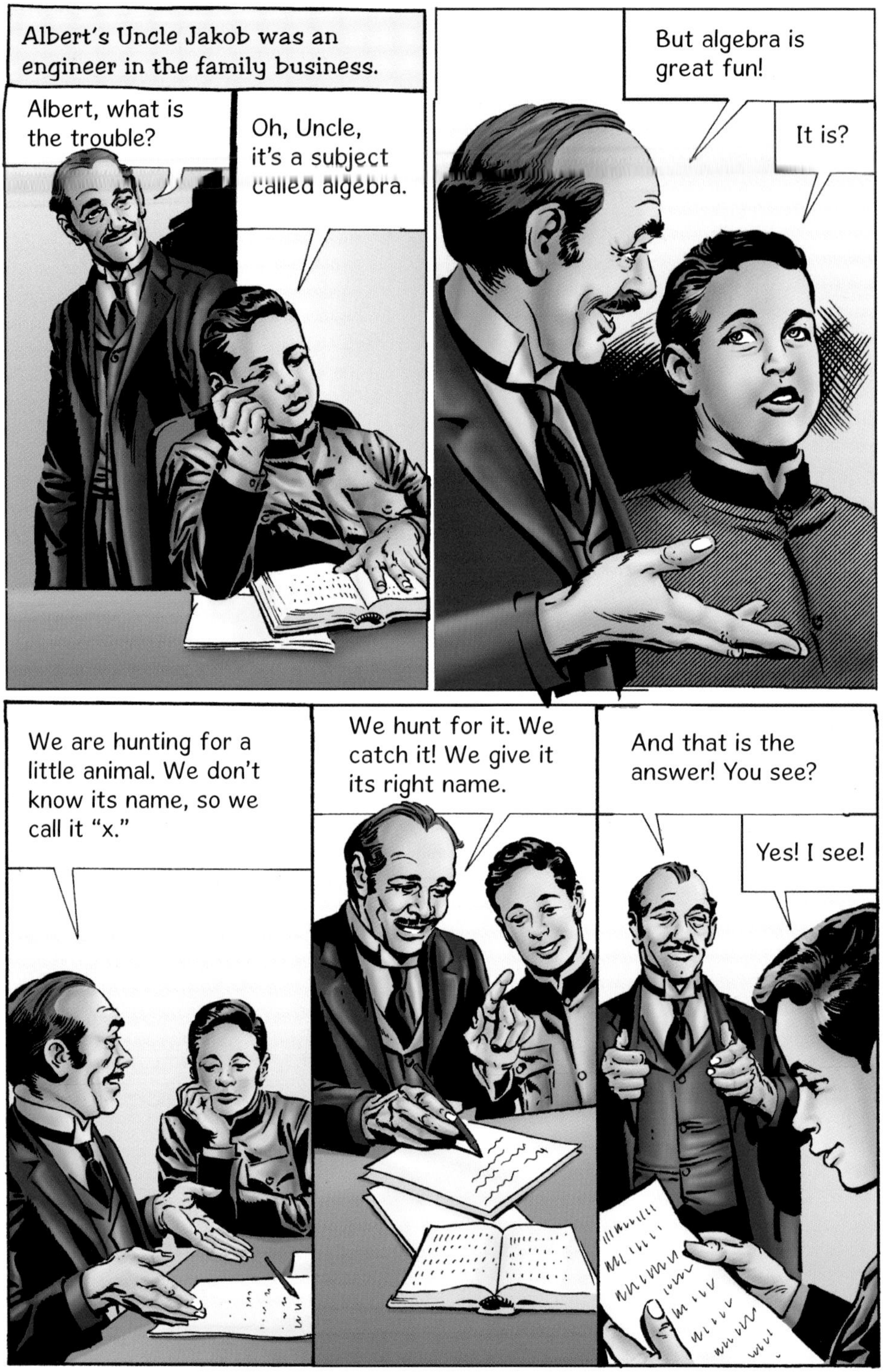
Albert's Uncle Jakob was an engineer in the family business.
Albert, what is the trouble?
Oh, Uncle, it's a subject called algebra.
But algebra is great fun!
It is?
We are hunting for a little animal. We don't know its name, so we call it "x."
We hunt for it. We catch it! We give it its right name.
And that is the answer! You see?
Yes! I see!

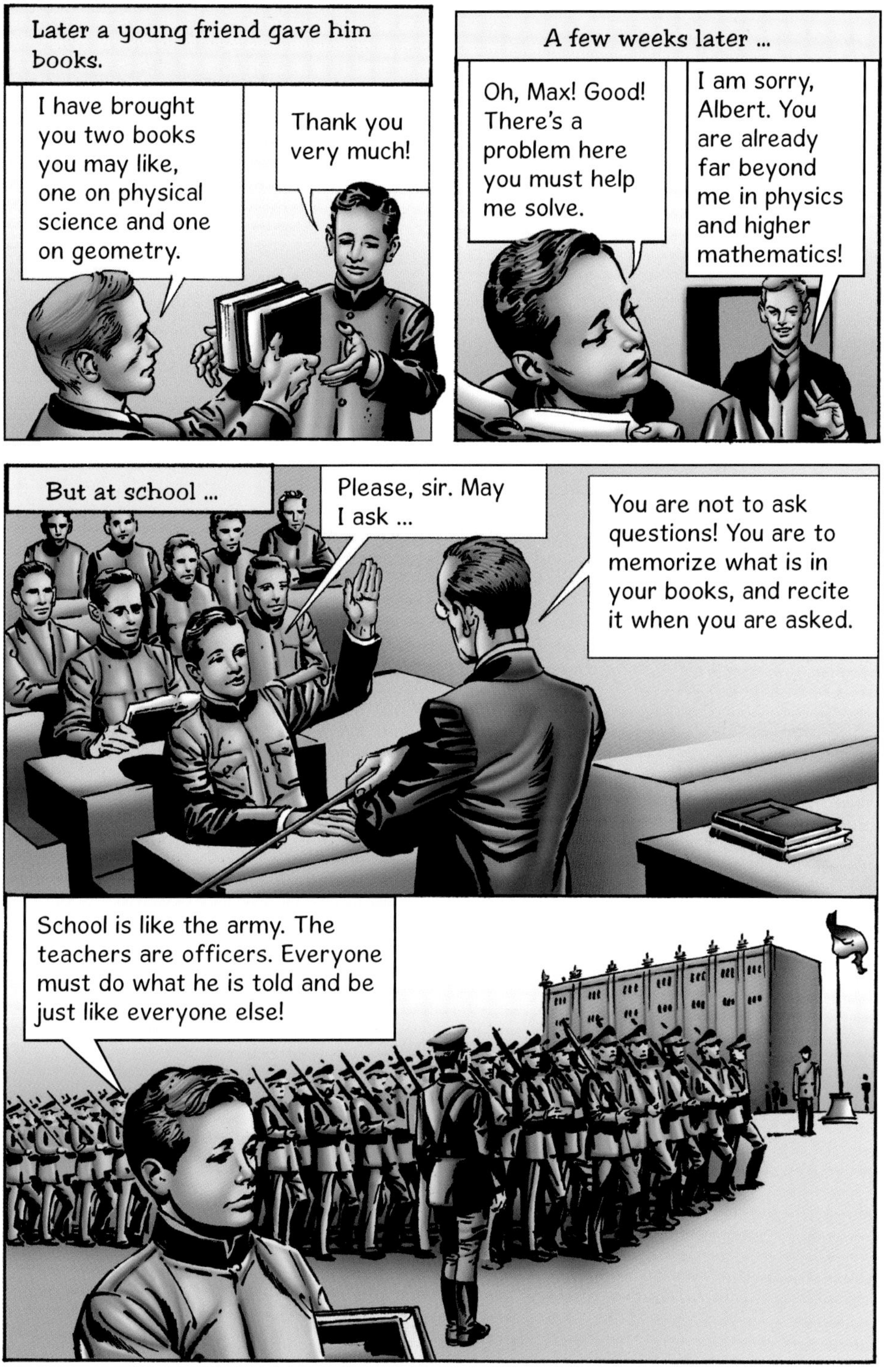
Later a young friend gave him books.
I have brought you two books you may like, one on physical science and one on geometry.
Thank you very much!
A few weeks later ...
Oh, Max! Good! There's a problem here you must help me solve.
I am sorry, Albert. You are already far beyond me in physics and higher mathematics!
But at school ...
Please, sir. May I ask ...
You are not to ask questions! You are to memorize what is in your books, and recite it when you are asked.
School is like the army. The teachers are officers. Everyone must do what he is told and be just like everyone else!

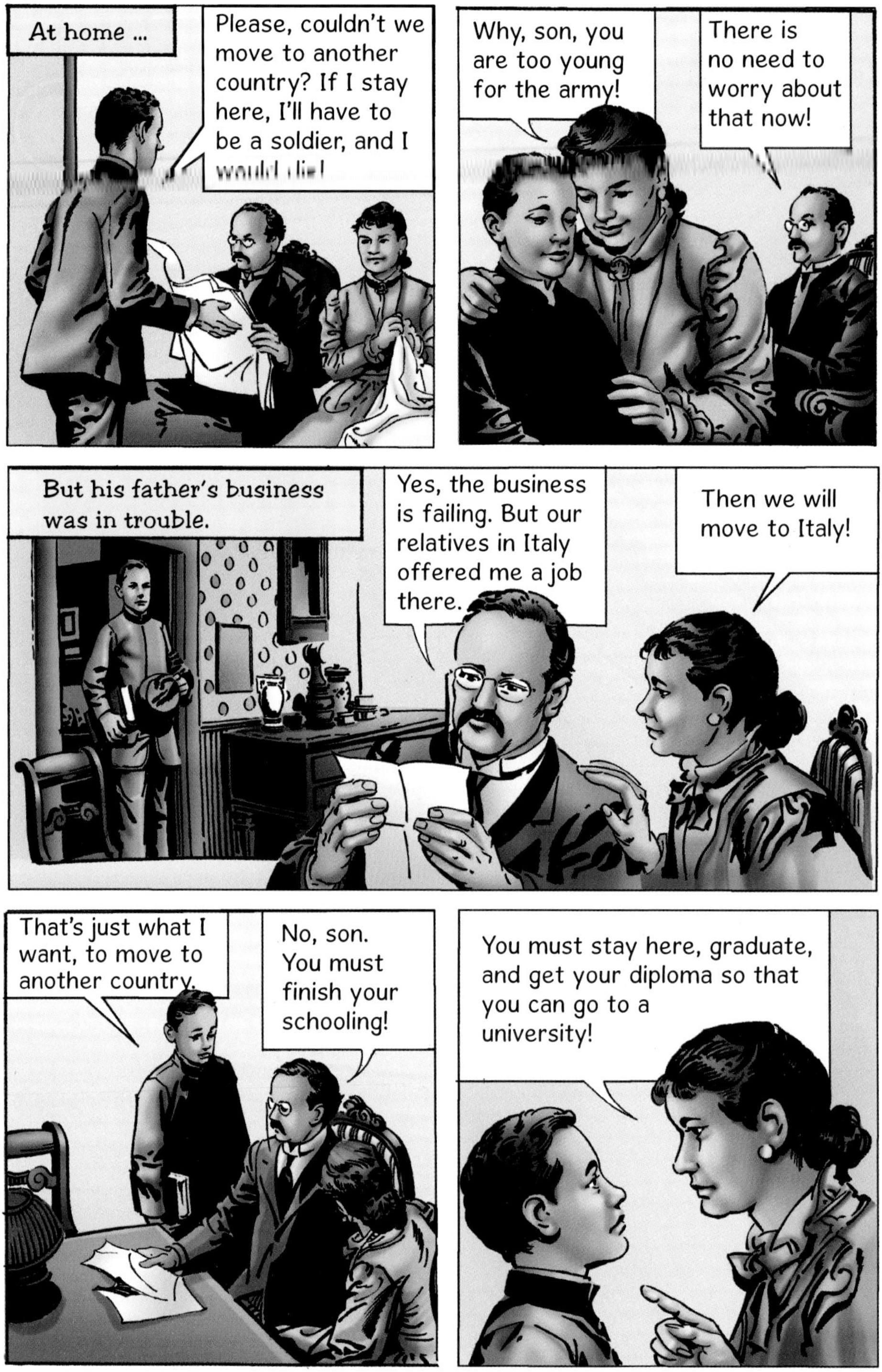
At home ...
Please, couldn't we move to another country? If I stay here, I'll have to be a soldier, and I would die!
Why, son, you are too young for the army!
There is no need to worry about that now!
But his father's business was in trouble.
Yes, the business is failing. But our relatives in Italy offered me a job there.
Then we will move to Italy!
That's just what I want, to move to another country.
No, son. You must finish your schooling!
You must stay here, graduate, and get your diploma so that you can go to a university!

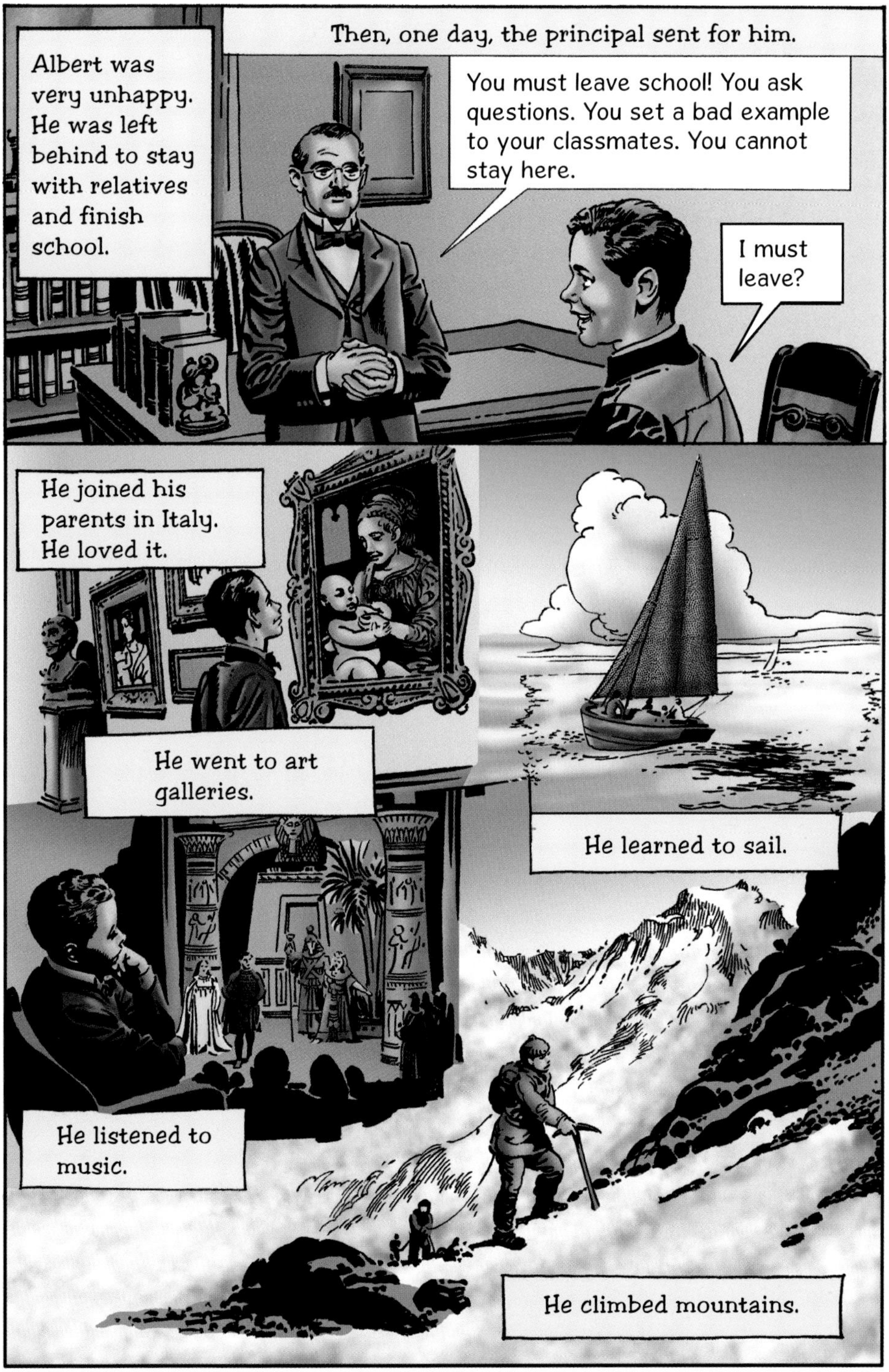
Albert was very unhappy. He was left behind to stay with relatives and finish school.
Then, one day, the principal sent for him.
You must leave school! You ask questions. You set a bad example to your classmates. You cannot stay here.
I must leave?
He joined his parents in Italy. He loved it.
He went to art galleries.
He learned to sail.
He listened to music.
He climbed mountains.

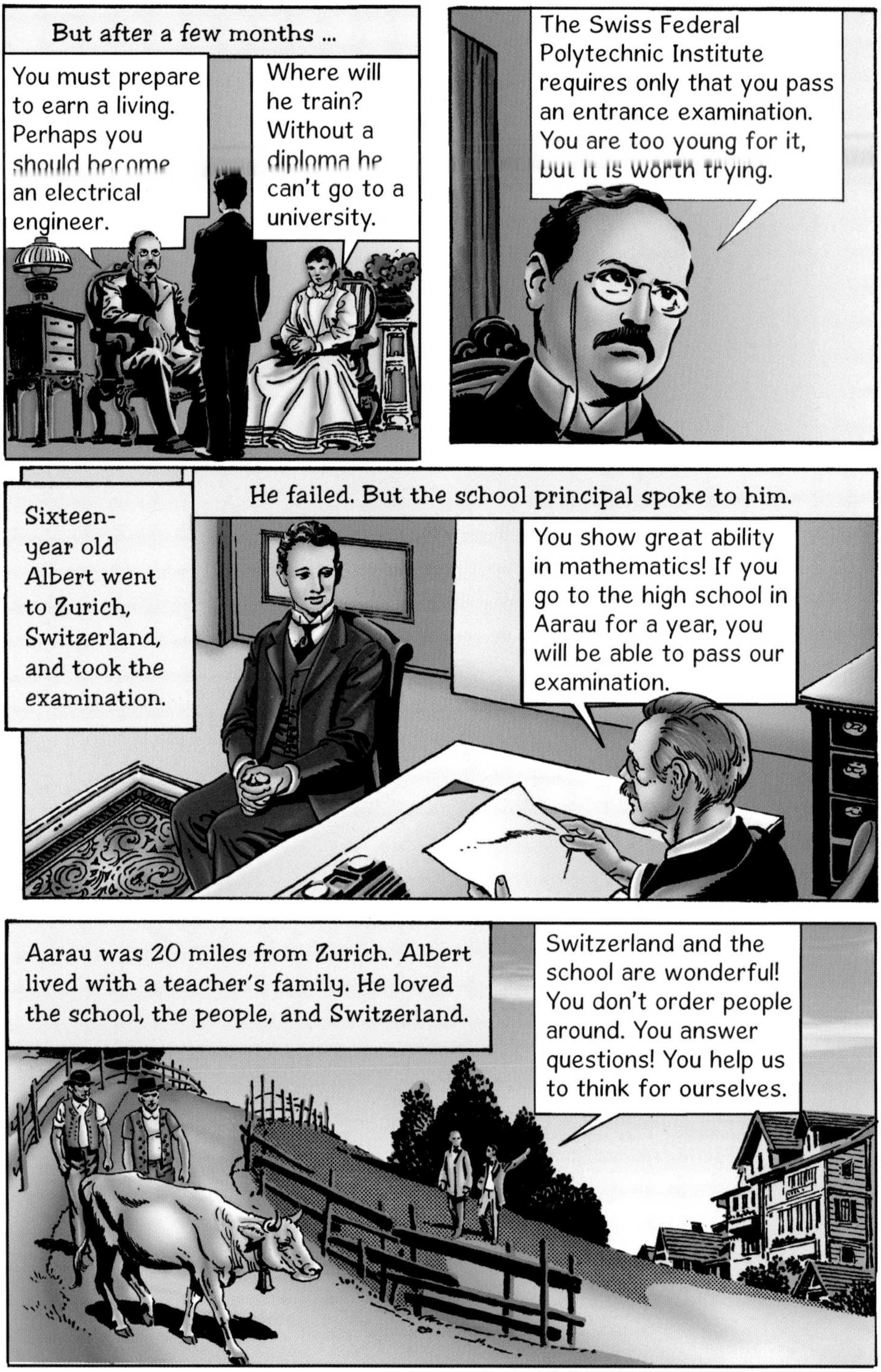
But after a few months ...
You must prepare to earn a living. Perhaps you should become an electrical engineer.
Where will he train? Without a diploma he can't go to a university.
The Swiss Federal Polytechnic Institute requires only that you pass an entrance examination. You are too young for it, but it is worth trying.
Sixteen-year old Albert went to Zurich, Switzerland, and took the examination.
He failed. But the school principal spoke to him.
You show great ability in mathematics! If you go to the high school in Aarau for a year, you will be able to pass our examination.
Aarau was 20 miles from Zurich. Albert lived with a teacher's family. He loved the school, the people, and Switzerland.
Switzerland and the school are wonderful! You don't order people around. You answer questions! You help us to think for ourselves.

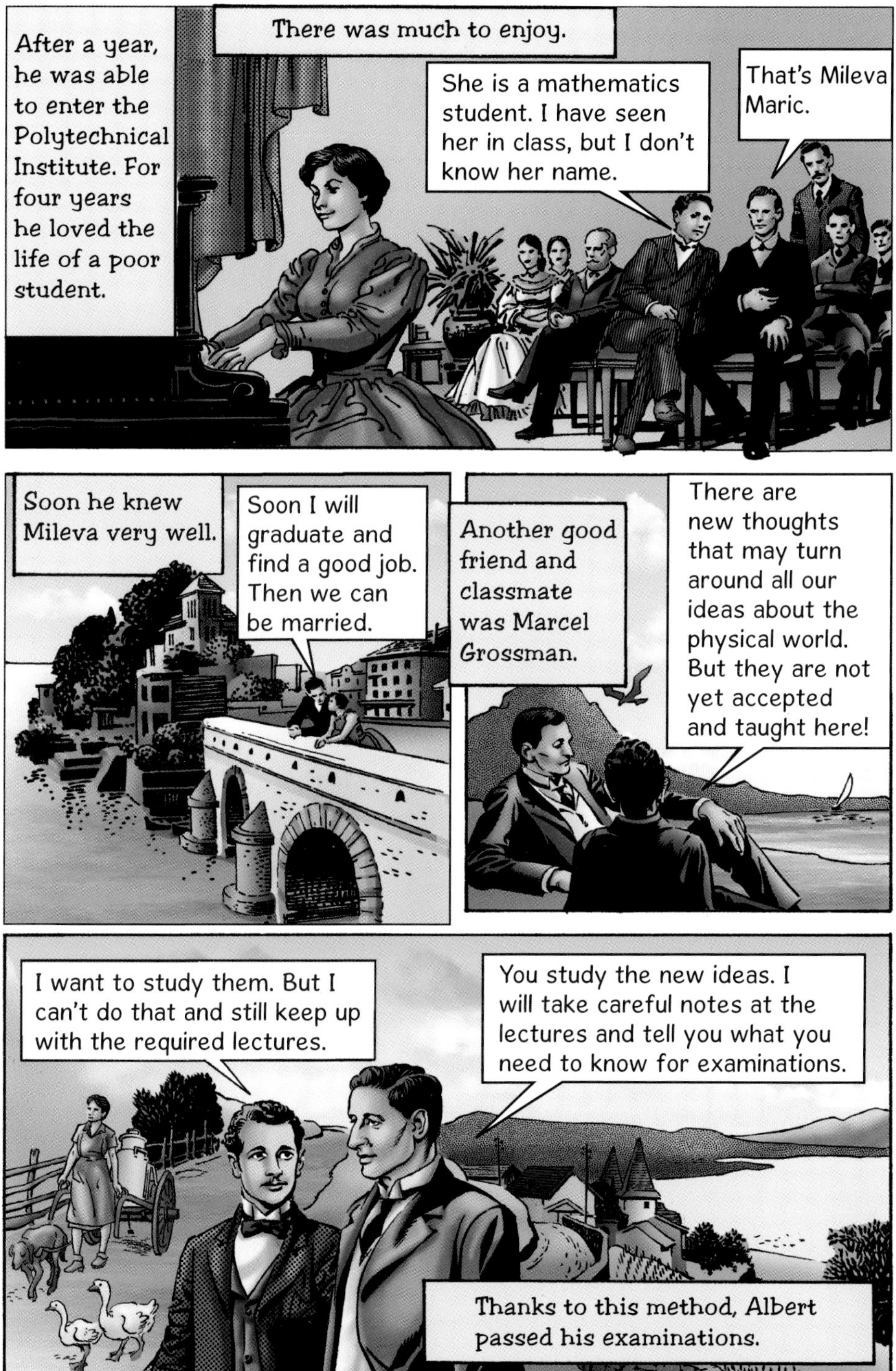
After a year, he was able to enter the Polytechnical Institute. For four years he loved the life of a poor student.
There was much to enjoy.
She is a mathematics student. I have seen her in class, but I don't know her name.
That's Mileva Maric.
Soon he knew Mileva very well.
Soon I will graduate and find a good job. Then we can be married.
Another good friend and classmate was Marcel Grossman.
There are new thoughts that may turn around all our ideas about the physical world. But they are not yet accepted and taught here!
I want to study them. But I can't do that and still keep up with the required lectures.
You study the new ideas. I will take careful notes at the lectures and tell you what you need to know for examinations.
Thanks to this method, Albert passed his examinations.

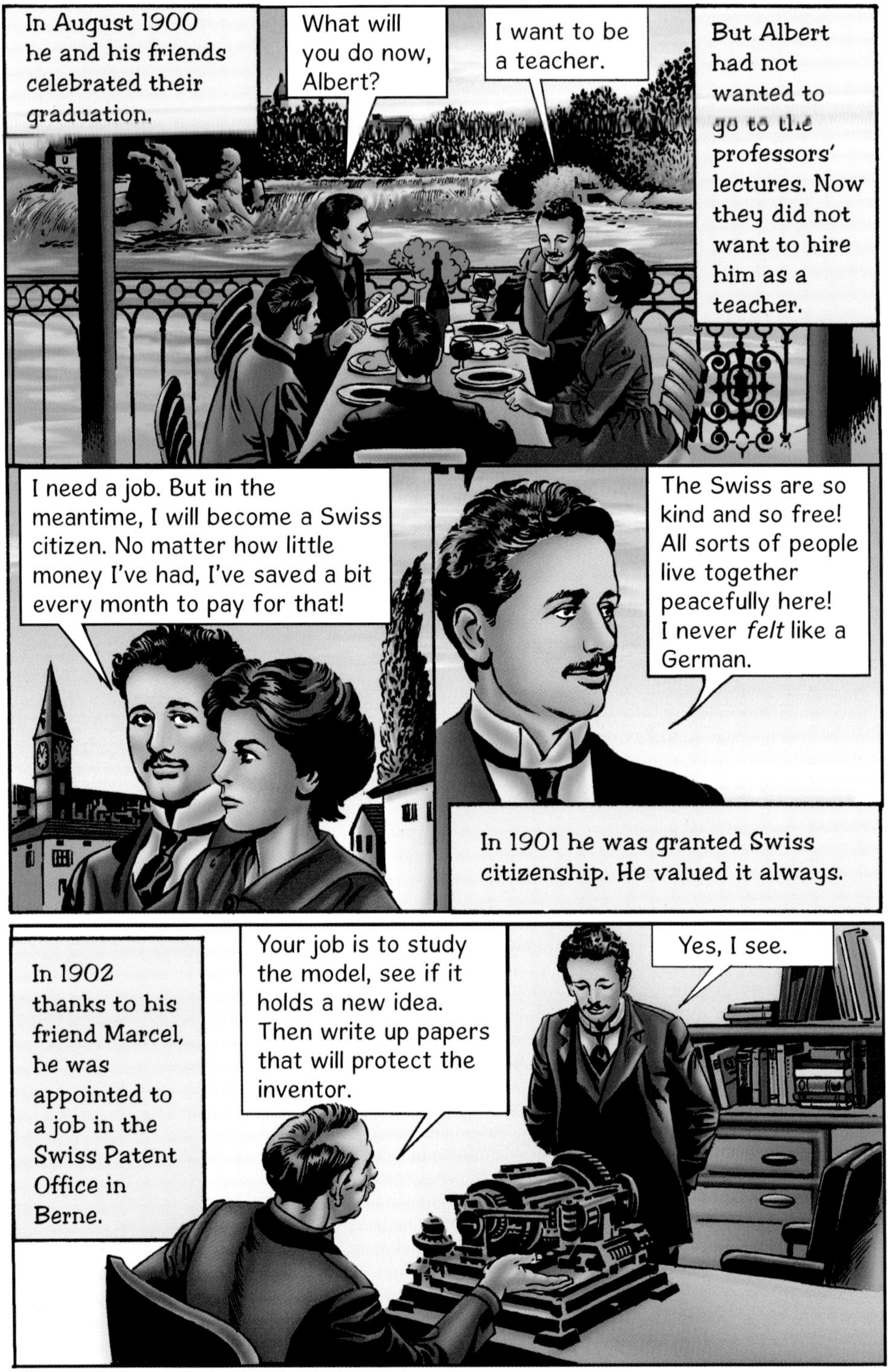
In August 1900 he and his friends celebrated their graduation.
What will you do now, Albert?
I want to be a teacher.
But Albert had not wanted to go to the professors' lectures. Now they did not want to hire him as a teacher.
I need a job. But in the meantime, I will become a Swiss citizen. No matter how little money I've had, I've saved a bit every month to pay for that!
The Swiss are so kind and so free! All sorts of people live together peacefully here! I never *felt* like a German.
In 1901 he was granted Swiss citizenship. He valued it always.
In 1902 thanks to his friend Marcel, he was appointed to a job in the Swiss Patent Office in Berne.
Your job is to study the model, see if it holds a new idea. Then write up papers that will protect the inventor.
Yes, I see.

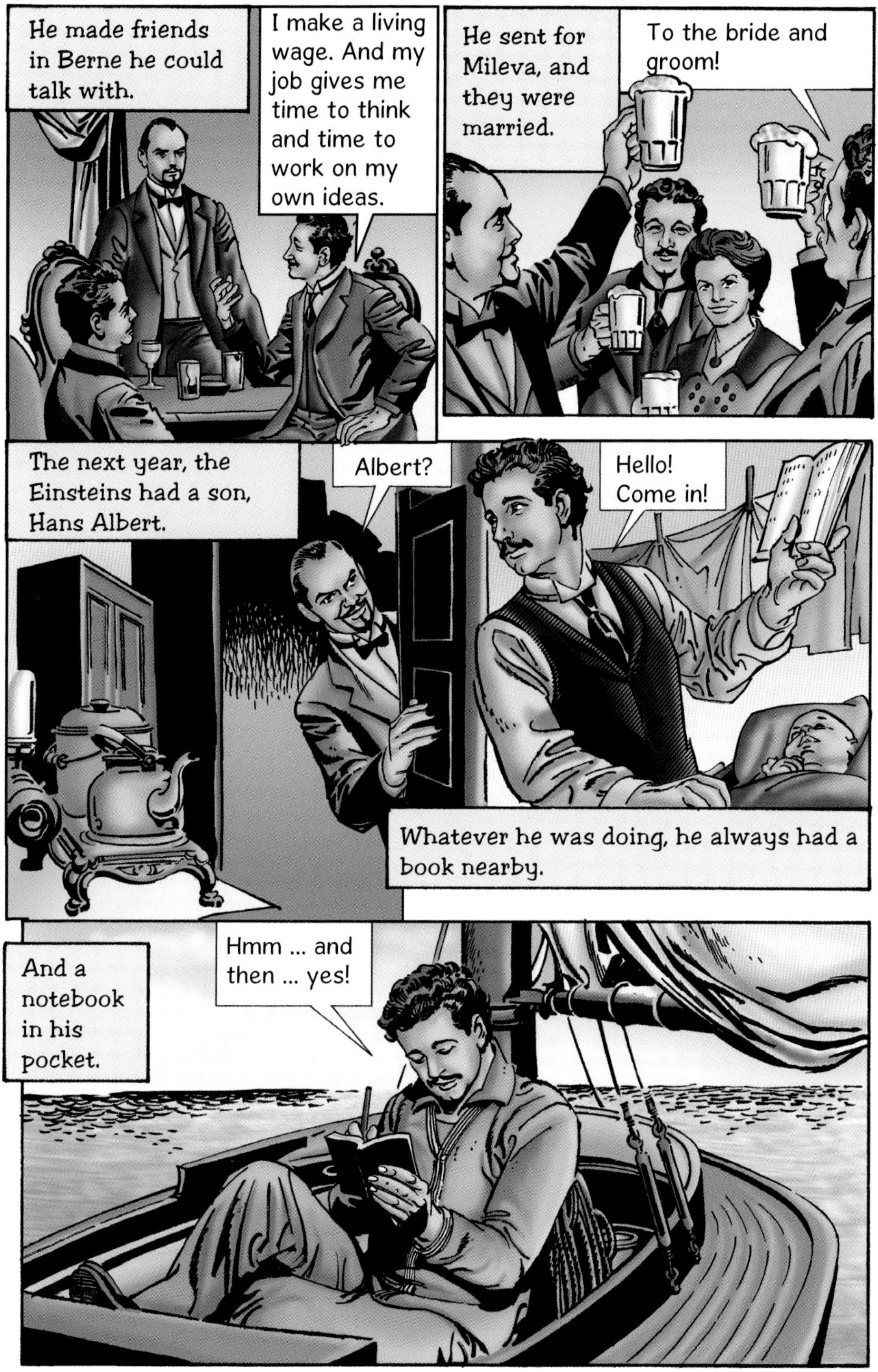
He made friends in Berne he could talk with.
I make a living wage. And my job gives me time to think and time to work on my own ideas.
He sent for Mileva, and they were married.
To the bride and groom!
The next year, the Einsteins had a son, Hans Albert.
Albert?
Hello! Come in!
Whatever he was doing, he always had a book nearby.
And a notebook in his pocket.
Hmm ... and then ... yes!

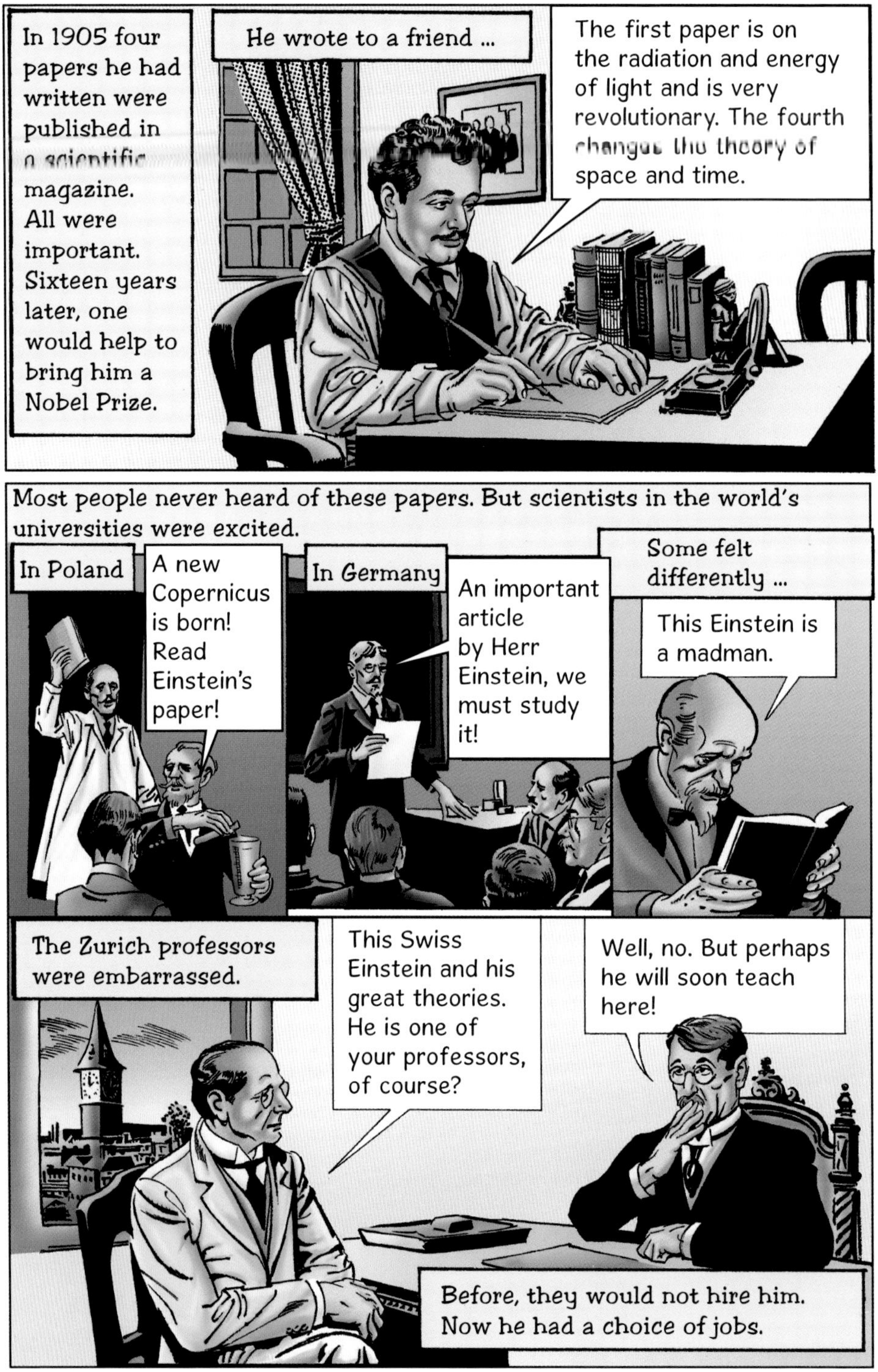
In 1905 four papers he had written were published in a scientific magazine. All were important. Sixteen years later, one would help to bring him a Nobel Prize.
He wrote to a friend ...
The first paper is on the radiation and energy of light and is very revolutionary. The fourth changes the theory of space and time.
Most people never heard of these papers. But scientists in the world's universities were excited.
In Poland
A new Copernicus is born! Read Einstein's paper!
In Germany
An important article by Herr Einstein, we must study it!
Some felt differently ...
This Einstein is a madman.
The Zurich professors were embarrassed.
This Swiss Einstein and his great theories. He is one of your professors, of course?
Well, no. But perhaps he will soon teach here!
Before, they would not hire him. Now he had a choice of jobs.

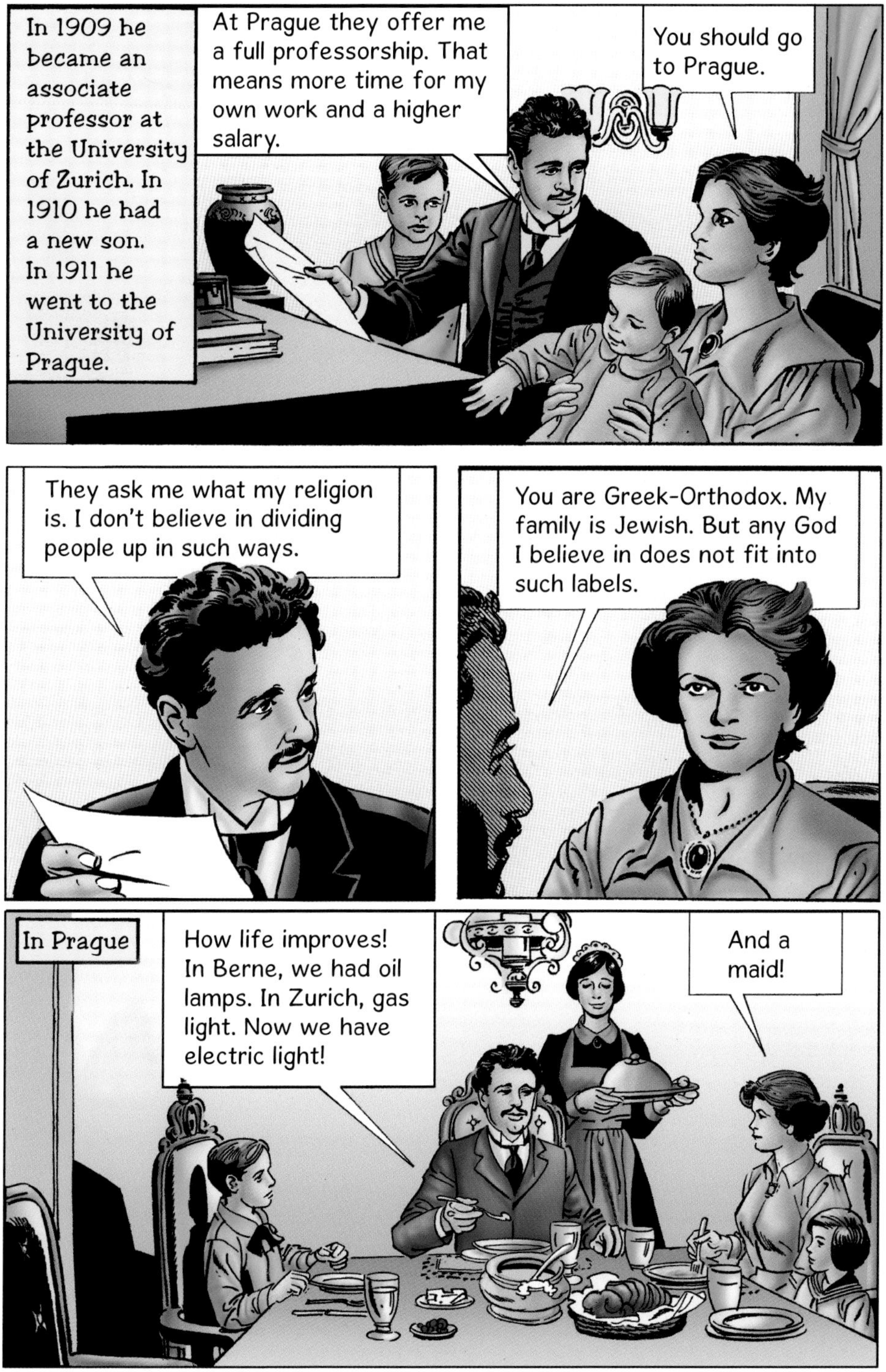
In 1909 he became an associate professor at the University of Zurich. In 1910 he had a new son. In 1911 he went to the University of Prague.
At Prague they offer me a full professorship. That means more time for my own work and a higher salary.
You should go to Prague.
They ask me what my religion is. I don't believe in dividing people up in such ways.
You are Greek-Orthodox. My family is Jewish. But any God I believe in does not fit into such labels.
In Prague
How life improves! In Berne, we had oil lamps. In Zurich, gas light. Now we have electric light!
And a maid!

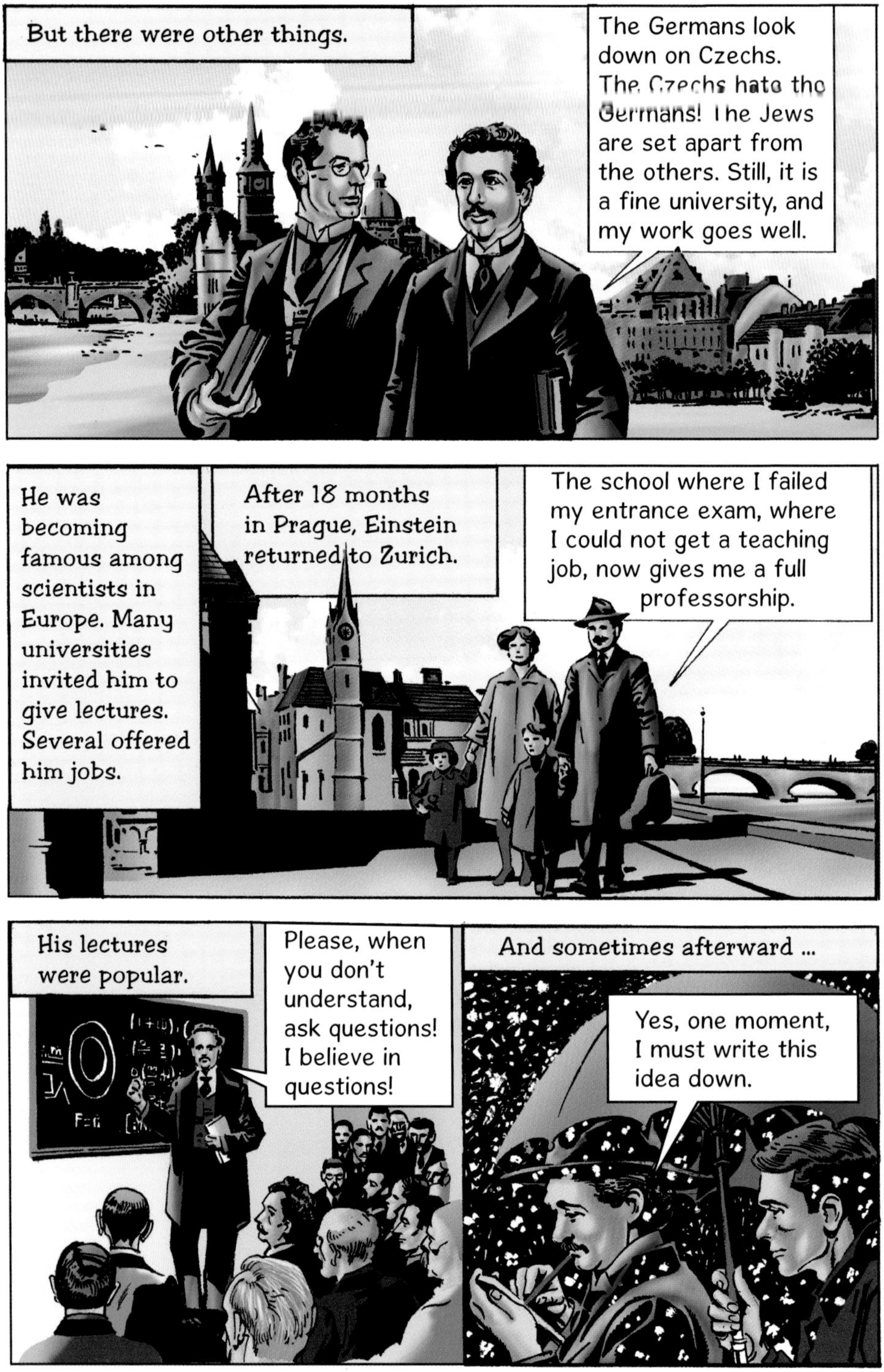
But there were other things.
The Germans look down on Czechs. The Czechs hate the Germans! The Jews are set apart from the others. Still, it is a fine university, and my work goes well.
He was becoming famous among scientists in Europe. Many universities invited him to give lectures. Several offered him jobs.
After 18 months in Prague, Einstein returned to Zurich.
The school where I failed my entrance exam, where I could not get a teaching job, now gives me a full professorship.
His lectures were popular.
Please, when you don't understand, ask questions! I believe in questions!
And sometimes afterward ...
Yes, one moment, I must write this idea down.

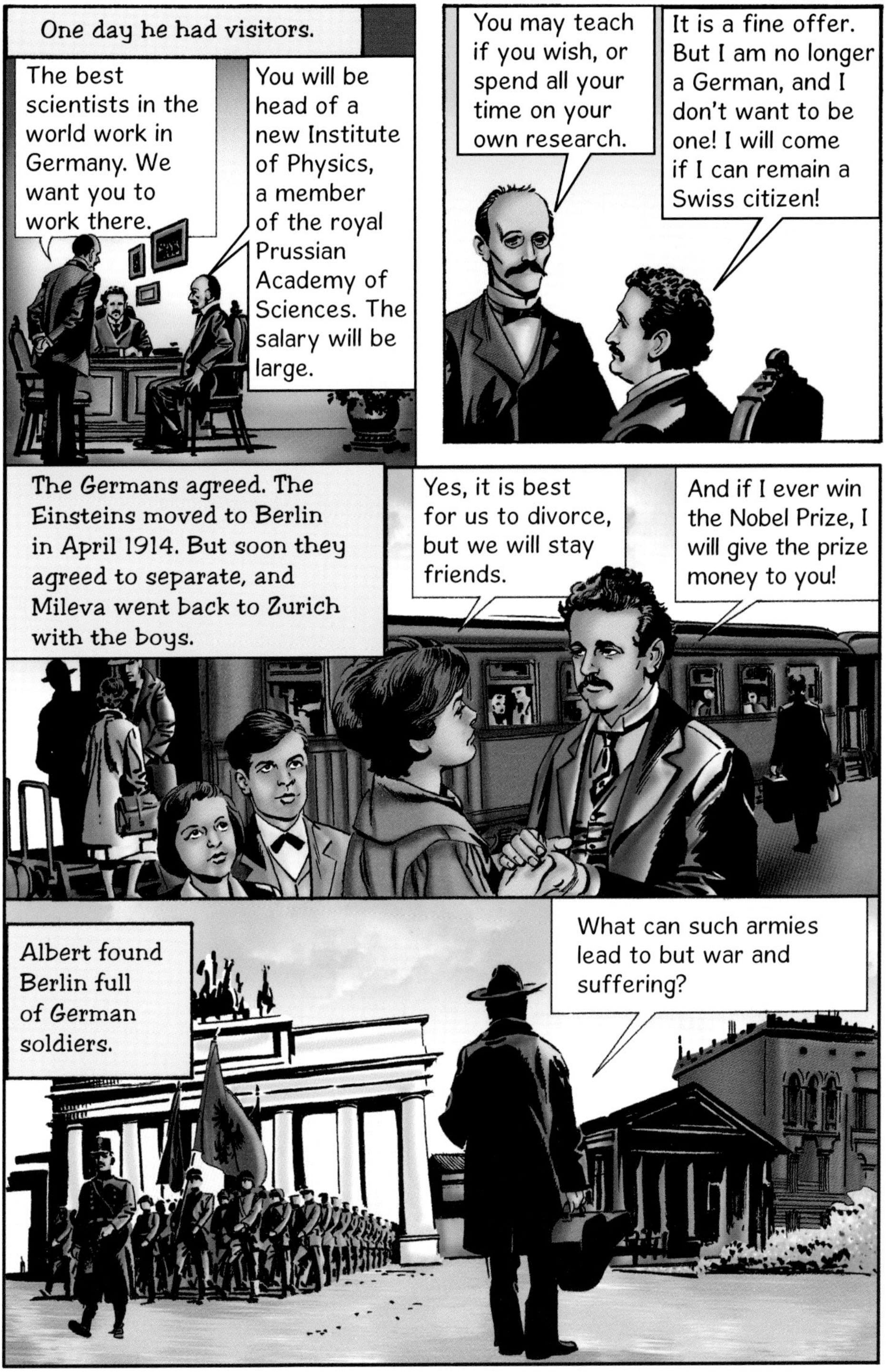
One day he had visitors.
The best scientists in the world work in Germany. We want you to work there.
You will be head of a new Institute of Physics, a member of the royal Prussian Academy of Sciences. The salary will be large.
You may teach if you wish, or spend all your time on your own research.
It is a fine offer. But I am no longer a German, and I don't want to be one! I will come if I can remain a Swiss citizen!
The Germans agreed. The Einsteins moved to Berlin in April 1914. But soon they agreed to separate, and Mileva went back to Zurich with the boys.
Yes, it is best for us to divorce, but we will stay friends.
And if I ever win the Nobel Prize, I will give the prize money to you!
Albert found Berlin full of German soldiers.
What can such armies lead to but war and suffering?

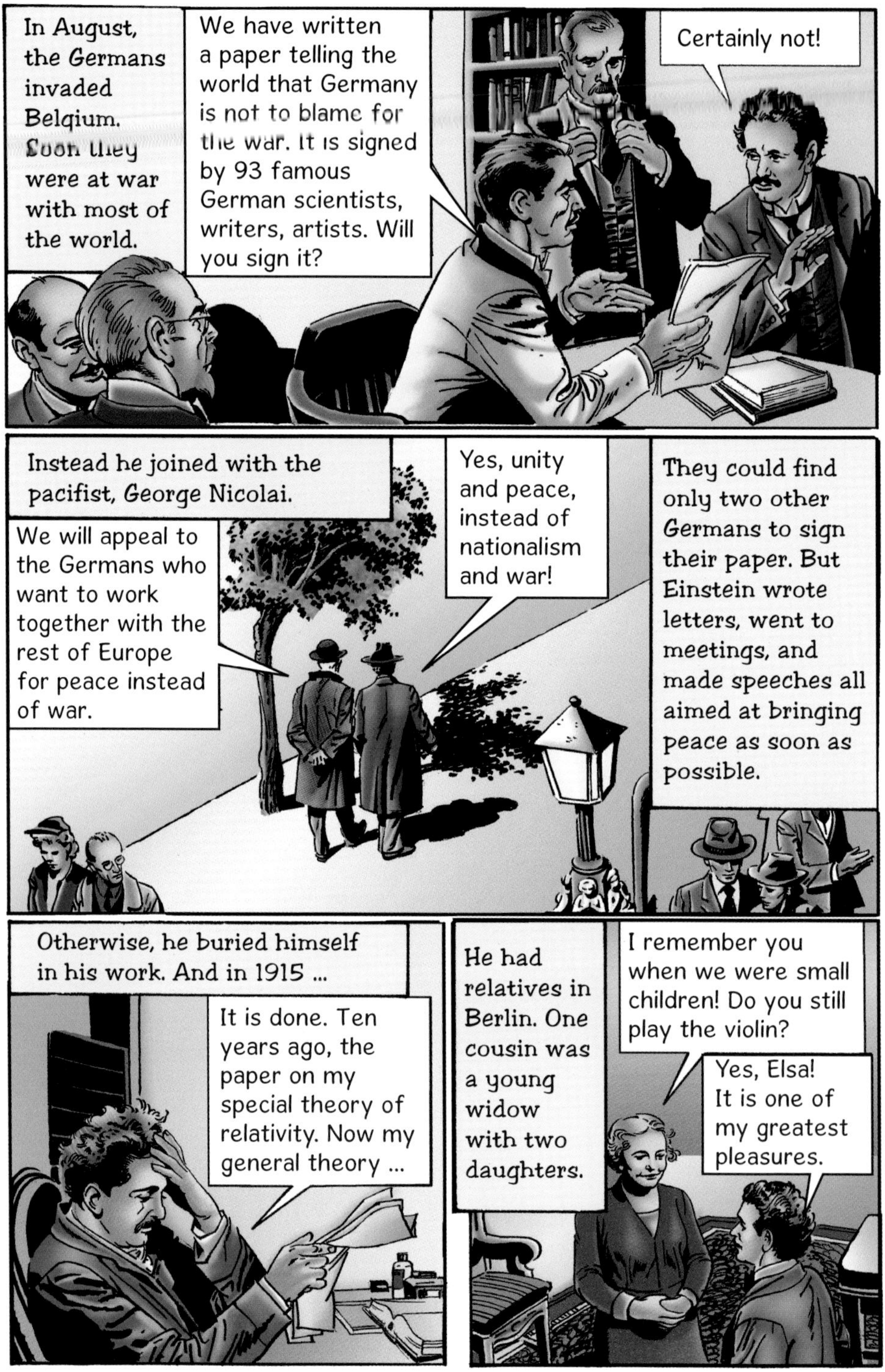
In August, the Germans invaded Belgium. Soon they were at war with most of the world.
We have written a paper telling the world that Germany is not to blame for the war. It is signed by 93 famous German scientists, writers, artists. Will you sign it?
Certainly not!
Instead he joined with the pacifist, George Nicolai.
We will appeal to the Germans who want to work together with the rest of Europe for peace instead of war.
Yes, unity and peace, instead of nationalism and war!
They could find only two other Germans to sign their paper. But Einstein wrote letters, went to meetings, and made speeches all aimed at bringing peace as soon as possible.
Otherwise, he buried himself in his work. And in 1915 ...
It is done. Ten years ago, the paper on my special theory of relativity. Now my general theory ...
He had relatives in Berlin. One cousin was a young widow with two daughters.
I remember you when we were small children! Do you still play the violin?
Yes, Elsa! It is one of my greatest pleasures.

In 1918 Germany surrendered and the war ended. In 1919 Albert and Elsa were married.

My theory holds that light traveling from the stars to earth will be bent as it passes near sun. So the stars will look to us as if they have moved out of place.

This could be proved during a total eclipse of the sun, when the stars would show up in the daytime.

Other scientists wanted to test Einstein's theories. In England ...

If we have people in Brazil and at Principe Island off South Africa, we should get fine views of a total eclipse.

We'll do it!

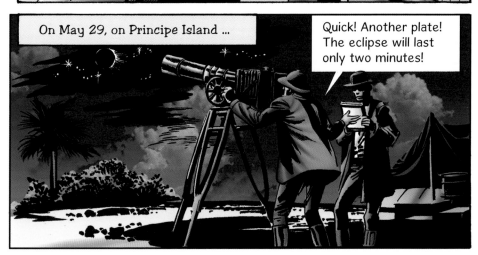

On May 29, on Principe Island ...

Quick! Another plate! The eclipse will last only two minutes!

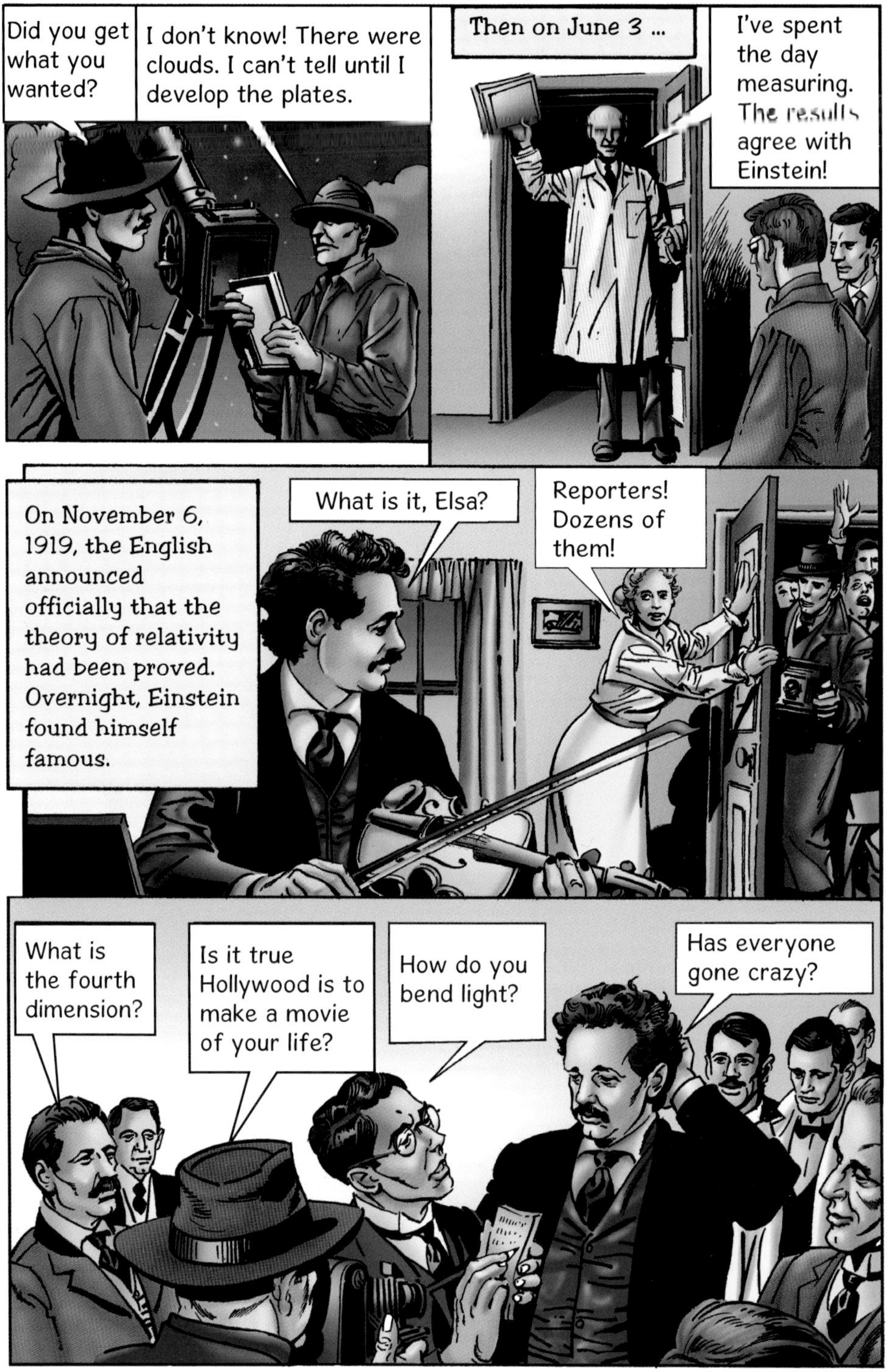
Did you get what you wanted?
I don't know! There were clouds. I can't tell until I develop the plates.
Then on June 3 ...
I've spent the day measuring. The results agree with Einstein!
On November 6, 1919, the English announced officially that the theory of relativity had been proved. Overnight, Einstein found himself famous.
What is it, Elsa?
Reporters! Dozens of them!
What is the fourth dimension?
Is it true Hollywood is to make a movie of your life?
How do you bend light?
Has everyone gone crazy?

There was mail from all over the world.

But what will I do with it?

There's a lot more outside!

And when he went out ...

Your autograph, Professor Einstein?

Don't move! I want your picture!

Scientists honored him, and he was offered jobs in many countries.

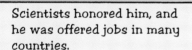

The more attention I receive, the more some Germans hate me! Because I am a Jew. Because I am a pacifist. Perhaps I should leave Germany.

The attacks on you are shameful, but only by riff-raff. We need you in Germany!

Yes, now that Germany is a republic, there is new hope for peace in Europe! I will stay and help!

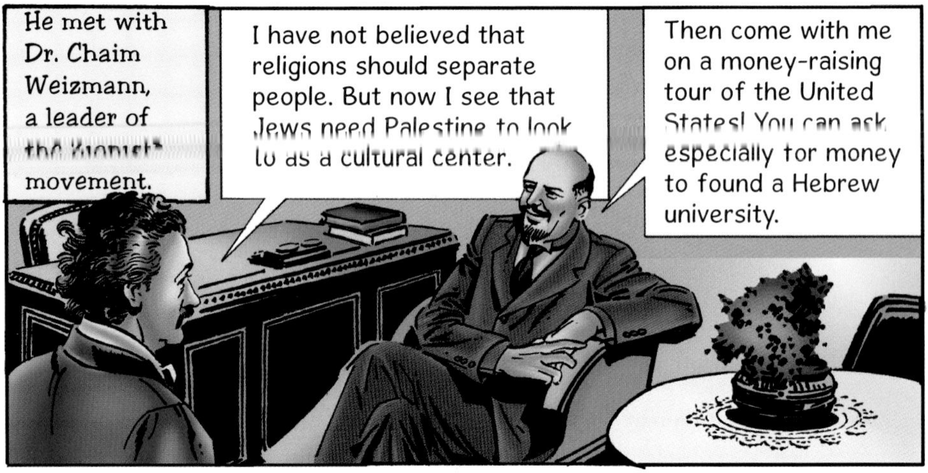
He met with Dr. Chaim Weizmann, a leader of the Zionist* movement.
I have not believed that religions should separate people. But now I see that Jews need Palestine to look to as a cultural center.
Then come with me on a money-raising tour of the United States! You can ask especially for money to found a Hebrew university.

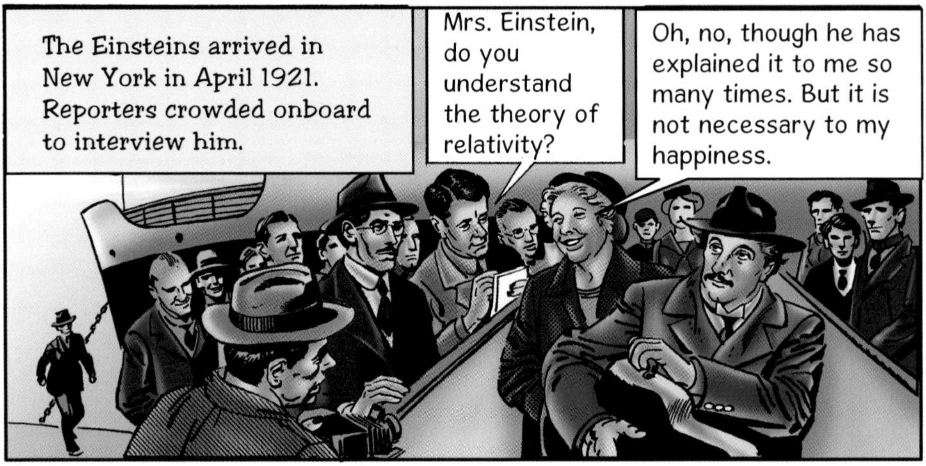
The Einsteins arrived in New York in April 1921. Reporters crowded onboard to interview him.
Mrs. Einstein, do you understand the theory of relativity?
Oh, no, though he has explained it to me so many times. But it is not necessary to my happiness.

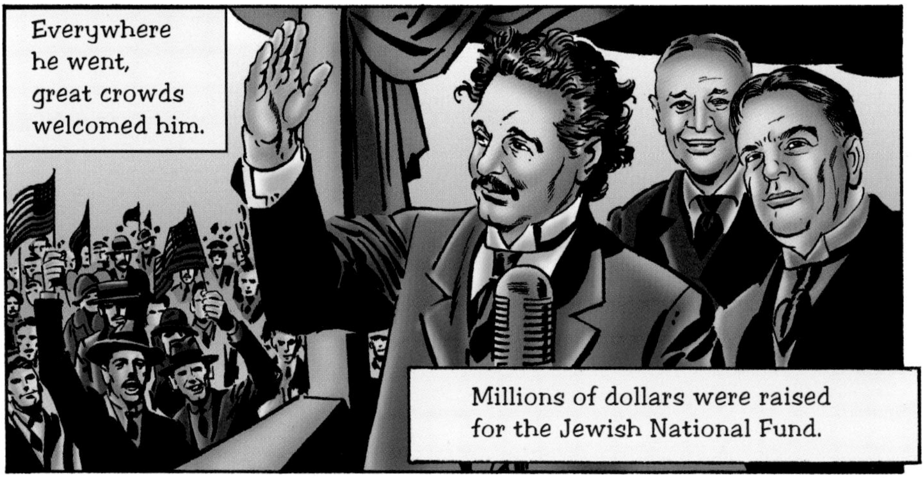
Everywhere he went, great crowds welcomed him.
Millions of dollars were raised for the Jewish National Fund.

* a Jewish movement in response to growing anti-Semitism that sought to reestablish a Jewish homeland in Palestine

He was invited to the White House. Columbia University gave him a medal. Princeton University gave him an honorary degree.

In the next few years, he would visit many countries. All over the world he was honored and loved.

Albert, you have won the Nobel Prize!

That's very nice! I promised to give the money to Mileva to educate my sons.

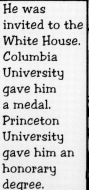

In Japan, a national holiday was held in his honor.

In one country only was he not honored. In Germany, Hitler and his followers blamed the Jews and Einstein for all their troubles.

Albert, please leave Germany! These Nazis have shot our great foreign minister, Dr. Rathenau. They threaten to kill you!

The Nazi party is only a small part of Germany. I must stay here and help to defeat them.

22

But in the next ten years, the Nazi party in Germany grew stronger. And Einstein had a visitor from America.

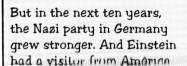

We are planning an institute of great scholars at Princeton, New Jersey. They would have no duties except to study and work as they wished. We would like you to be its head!

Perhaps, if I could spend a few months there each year.

His family and friends grew more afraid for his safety.

The Nazis grow more threatening every day.

They attack you by name. They call your theory of relativity a Jewish plot against the world!

There is a rumor that they have offered a $5,000 reward to anyone who will kill you!

I had not realized my head was worth so much!

Albert, it is no joke. Please, you must leave Germany!

We have a trip already planned. I'll go to the United States for a winter at the California Institute of Technology.

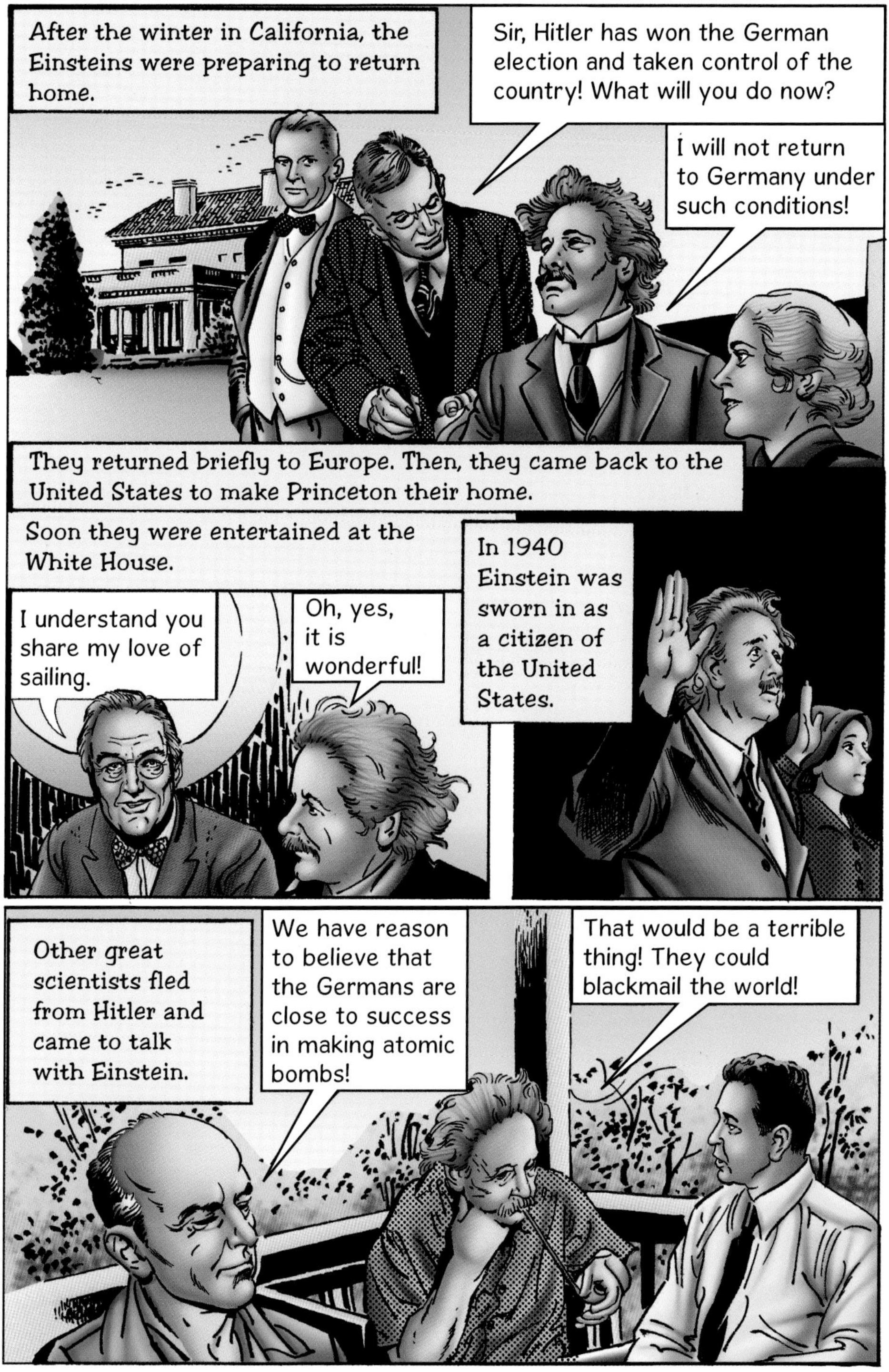
After the winter in California, the Einsteins were preparing to return home.
Sir, Hitler has won the German election and taken control of the country! What will you do now?
I will not return to Germany under such conditions!
They returned briefly to Europe. Then, they came back to the United States to make Princeton their home.
Soon they were entertained at the White House.
I understand you share my love of sailing.
Oh, yes, it is wonderful!
In 1940 Einstein was sworn in as a citizen of the United States.
Other great scientists fled from Hitler and came to talk with Einstein.
We have reason to believe that the Germans are close to success in making atomic bombs!
That would be a terrible thing! They could blackmail the world!

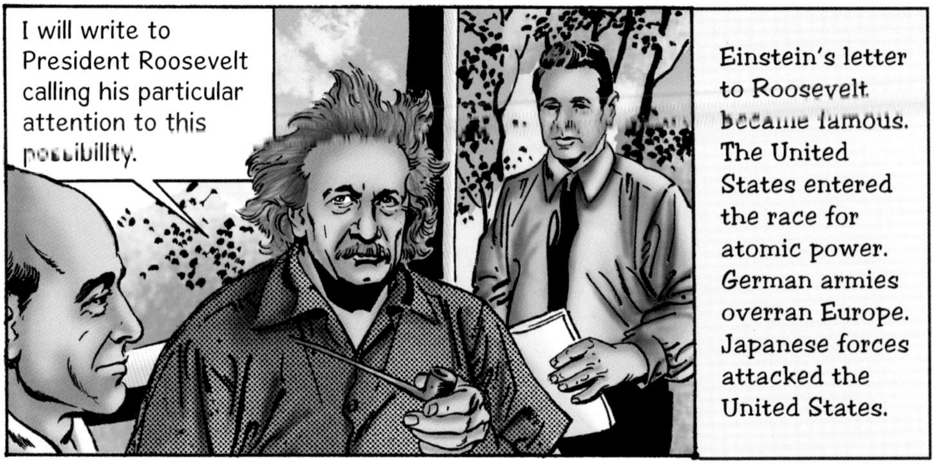
I will write to President Roosevelt calling his particular attention to this possibility.
Einstein's letter to Roosevelt became famous. The United States entered the race for atomic power. German armies overran Europe. Japanese forces attacked the United States.

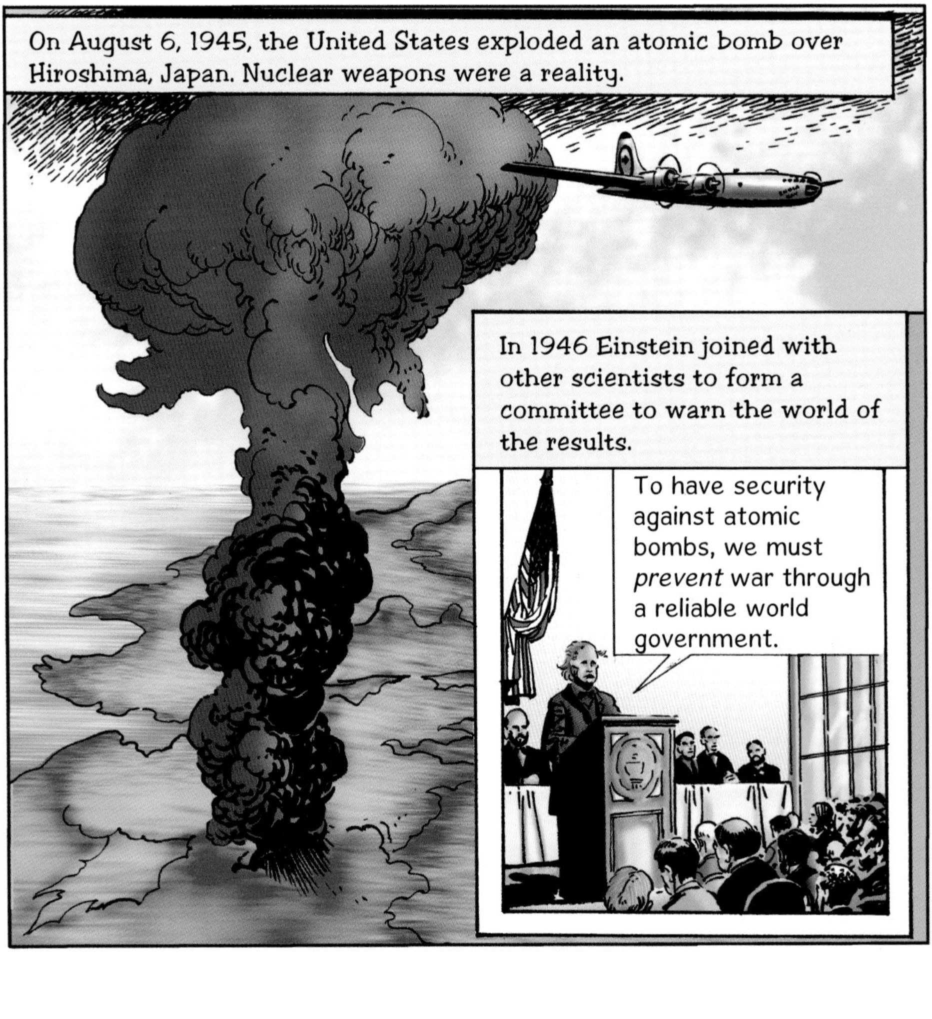
On August 6, 1945, the United States exploded an atomic bomb over Hiroshima, Japan. Nuclear weapons were a reality.
In 1946 Einstein joined with other scientists to form a committee to warn the world of the results.
To have security against atomic bombs, we must *prevent* war through a reliable world government.

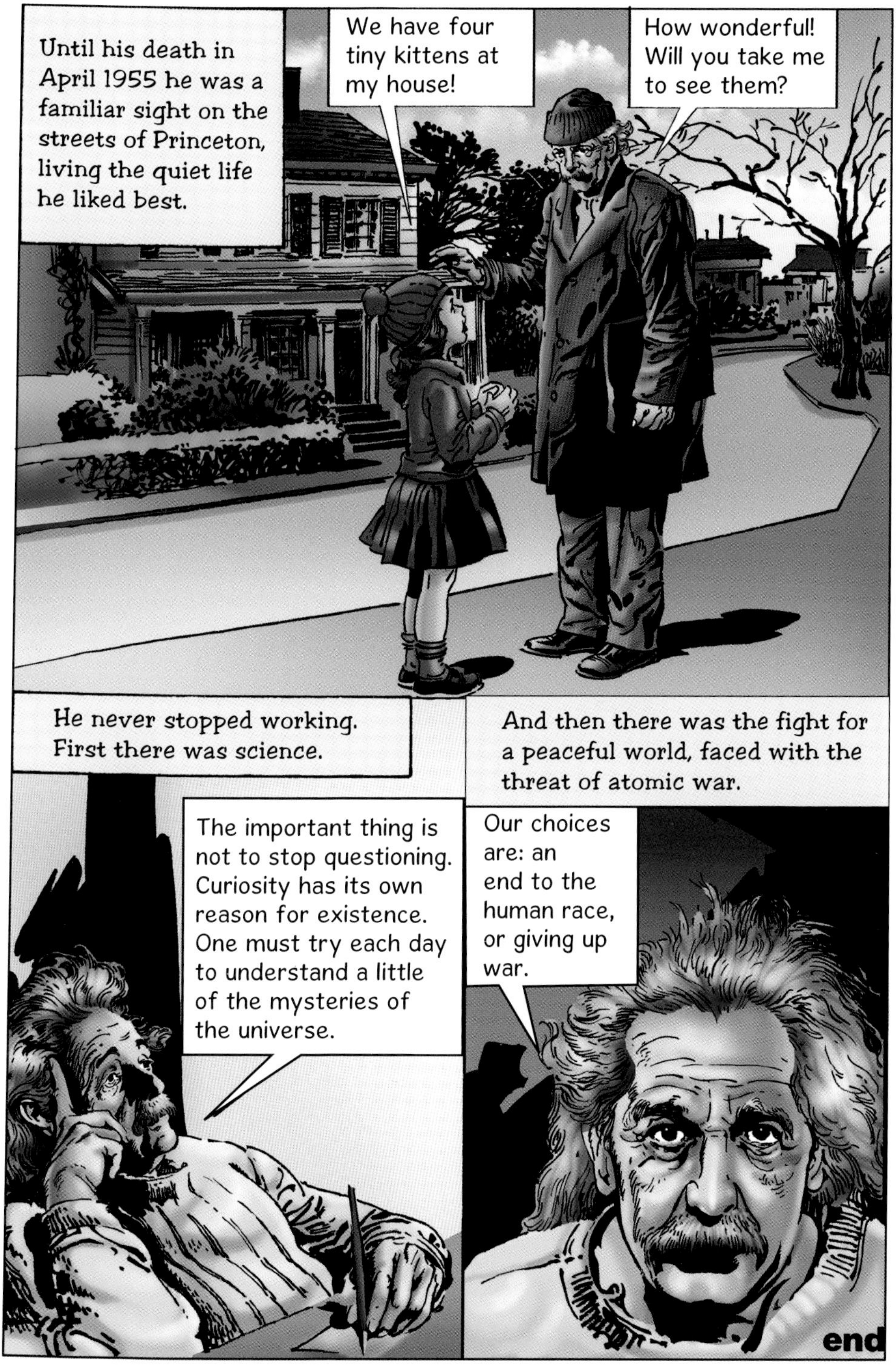
Until his death in April 1955 he was a familiar sight on the streets of Princeton, living the quiet life he liked best.
We have four tiny kittens at my house!
How wonderful! Will you take me to see them?
He never stopped working. First there was science.
The important thing is not to stop questioning. Curiosity has its own reason for existence. One must try each day to understand a little of the mysteries of the universe.
And then there was the fight for a peaceful world, faced with the threat of atomic war.
Our choices are: an end to the human race, or giving up war.
end